Moon Chaser

Running from the Sun

ISBN-10: 0692077642
ISBN-13: 978-0-692-07764-1

Dedicated
To
All of those who have stood
by me through my worst.

Only when the night falls,
moonlight casts your shadow,
it hovers over me so aggressively.
Take your days out on me, please.
You are my most successful nothing,
yet the crutch I lean on.

Undressing me is such a turn-on
as each article of clothing falls,
I just stand in front of you with nothing
but a desiring shadow.
You always aim to please,
touching my body so aggressively.

"Don't mind if I hit it aggressively,"
you say as you climb on.
"Do as you please,"
I whisper as my body falls
to the bed as you cling to my shadow.
So subtly, I am more to you than nothing.

I want to feel all rather than nothing,
so give it to me more aggressively.
Cause the screams to come from my shadow
as you put me on.
Darkness opens as rain falls,
begging you to continue, please.

You want me to beg you more, please,
for the something that is my nothing
as long as neither heart falls.
You grab my hips aggressively,
continuously turning me on
as I watch our bodies in the shadow.

Light rises, slowly fading the shadow,
yet we are both satisfied to do as we please.
It's time to put our clothes back on
and retreat to what we have told ourselves is nothing.
"Sorry if I was too aggressive, Lee."
"It's okay, only when the night falls."

I loved you but it was brief.
I would have told you
but you might have loved me too,
and I couldn't let you do that.

Instead I was your hero,
saving you from me.
And all that time,
you had no idea
that I adored you.

So when you think
she doesn't love you,
remember that she does.

Don't let her be your hero,
she is the one that needs saving.
Show her that you love her
even when she doesn't
because sometimes
the strongest guard protects the weakest wall.

Is it desperation
to want someone to love?
Is it mere selfishness
to want to be loved?

During this era,
where all souls
are often broken,
is it too much to ask,
for love?

Should I be
embarrassed
searching the surface,
yearning for the genuine
connection?

Ready to endure
what binds us together
what tears us apart.
Do I hide
because I am
ready?

Or can I embrace
the next chapter,
confidently turn
the page,
absorb the letters
that define this love?

Is it weak
to give love
another chance?
Will you open
the book
for the answer
or burn the paper?

You.
I can't wait to love you
for you
and all puzzle pieces
that are missing
to ones that fit.
For the musky moments
of man
weathered and rugged.

Me.
You can't wait to love me
for the over-filled
basket case
of dirty laundry.
For the fresh, clean scent
of woman after a scalding
hot shower.

We.
Once upon a time
when the story told,
stars
you
and
me.

It is the story often-told
of a girl so desperate to love
inside of a woman afraid,
to feel.

She is waiting for him
to show her the world
in all the ways she never saw.

Idly, she impatiently waits
until he reaches his hand
to place inside hers.

She knows the kind
of simple love she wants
isn't so simple nowadays.

Through all the doubt,
she holds the slightest speck
of hope in her heart
and maybe, just maybe
he might
be waiting for her too.

You were the sunset;
your presence was brief
but bright.

As it became closer
to your departure,
your streaks of light
burst with purpose
through my ocean.

Night falls
and you are gone.
These days
the sun rises
without you.
And I am
supposed to be
okay.

I am not okay
and it isn't
because your light
is dim.

I am not okay
because my light
has yet to shine
upon my ocean
and reflect
on the edge
of my own waves.

I am not okay
because I still
depend
on the sun
to give me
the world.

When I should
have the world
as the gift
I gave myself.

Being in your embrace
feels hopelessly
hopeful.

I fall in love
with the brief
moments we share.

Each time we meet
is an opened bottle
of Merlot that I revisit
for a stemmed glass
of fantasy.

Drunk in your affection,
I fall for your charm.
Telling myself I won't
drink again,
but I'm addicted
to your encounter.

I don't have your love
as my drug
but your time
satisfies my craving.

As I sober up
from this stupor,
I've had my fix
until the next binge.

Either way
it's rehab
or
alcoholism
that will determine
our fate.

The night breathes
life between corners
of her window.

The stillness stain
against bedroom walls
bring sanctuary
to her trying mind.

Day in, day out,
a hope for bliss
met with the reality
of disruption.

Soul separation,
lifting above her body,
looking down
at what she has become.

She is a beauty
in her own decision,
a devil in her destruction.
A true force
that only the strong
can survive.

It will take a beast
of all beasts to conquer
the cardiac
of this passionate woman.

He looked into my eyes saying,
"I could choke you to death,
the crazy thing is,
I know you would let me."
I just went into this trance.

He continued, "So what's the point?"
He glided his fingers
around my neck and collar bone,
like I was an object that he owned.
He did own me.

I surrendered my body over and over.
There wasn't anything he couldn't do.
His hands graced my shoulder,
sliding my sleeve off, touching my breast.
He grabbed my neck so precisely.

Looking dead in my eyes,
I could feel him from underneath me.
I was at a loss for words.
All I could do is sit there
under his spell as he continued to take me.

Blood trickles down
edges of broken glass.
Risking a sip
from a rigged rim.

Full, supple lips
gently placed on
severed shards
of the half-full vessel.

Applying pressure,
afflicting her essence.
Drawing out vital fluids
that hide beneath
the surface.

Captivated by danger,
imperiling the organ
that thrives on agony.
Sabotage the skin
protecting her vulnerability.

Pierce through the shell
of uncertainty.
Turn her inside out,
desecrate what remains.

Nails scratch paths
across my back.
I submit to your travels
on, around and through
my body.

Every inch of me
is on the itinerary.
You are no tourist,
you've conquered
this vessel over and over.

Yet, there is more left
for your discovery.
I kneel before you,
great traveler.

Explore all unknown
depths of me,
touch upon
the untouched.

Uncover me,
Unearth me,
Discover me,
Take what is yours.

You know what's easier
than falling in love?
Dying.

When I start to feel
vulnerable, happy, secure;
I immediately feel like losing
control.

I want to give up
before he hurts me.
Before I realize
that I believed all the lies
just to have these precious
moments.

Drowning myself,
knowingly in all his tales
and convincing myself
that someone could be
genuine.

For once, I feel bonded,
in bondage,
for this love affair.
Rather than see it through,
I prefer to die.

I don't want to find out
this was all a Spanish lullaby.
I don't want to know
that it's a game.

Darkness. Silence.
Goodbye.

He's dangerous.
He's wrong.
He's every reason
to run away.

He's unstable
with his heart.
He's overthinking
with his mind.

He's all the mistakes
I have ever made,
perfectly tucked
in my bed.

He lives
beneath my skin,
runs chills
throughout my body.

He possesses
the fear
that nests
in the core
of my world.

I want to endure
all of his errors.
I am in love
with his disaster.

If I hide the bottle
behind the bar,
will anyone know
I've been drinking it?

You're my best kept
secret, whispering sweet
nothings close to my ear.
Your breath sends chills
down my spine, drunk.

They keep telling me
I have a problem,
I'm so addicted
to the taste of you.

Your label tells me
you're toxic
but I refuse to believe.
I keep you at room temperature
because I never want to feel
the cold on my tongue.

You're warm when I hold you,
you're there when I need you.
You're mine when we're drinking,
your bottle is half full when I'm thinking.

I can't stop reaching
for this glass of red,
stain my lips,
drown my mind
in your L....

Lust? Love?
Just drown me.
I don't want to know.

Vigorously wrestling with this lust
and the undeniable illusion of love.
An undying desire to change my mind,
for what sits inside is far too wrong
to ever be made right.
Still, I dig my nails into your body.

25 layers of lust
25 layers of love

Pour another glass,
lips to rim,
devour the taste
of you.

Ran from rehab
with just the hint
of intoxication.
Brain, washed down
potent liquor
to my core.

Drunk in lust
or love,
lines blurred,
obliterated sense
driven by desire.

Sobriety
was never meant
for me
so long as you ferment.

At first,
all I needed,
the vigorous touch,
to take me away.

Grounded
in this security,
it carried me
through time.

Your hand brushed
my hair behind my ear
in the early morning
and burdened my heart.

Now my hair flies free,
body untouched,
holding on to memories
only I can see.

An empty bottle
of red wine
stands alone
on my table.

What once was full
of exuberant
experiences
of our nothing,
is now recyclable
trash.

Left with the aftertaste
of late nights,
mindless connections,
extreme foreplay
towards disaster.

Withdrawal shreds
piece by piece
of mind and body.
Back to life,
the return to rehab.

Small spaces
that hide between
the day and the night,
the only time
I am allowed to keep
you.

Mid-night light
peeks in,
resting itself
on the hopeless.

We are but stars
in an endless sky
directed by chaos.
Riding through tides
of the moon.

Tell a tale,
to lessen pain,
to hide truth,
to repair bridges.

What do they want?
Hands pulling this body
under blinding waves.
Drowning,
survival of the fittest,
lunge this vessel up for air.

Gasp a saving breath
from wind of mistrust.
What lies ahead,
or what lie are you ahead of?

If the truth will set you free,
you will be encaged forever.

Tired but can't sleep,
hungry but can't eat,
thirsty but can't drink,
teary but can't blink.

Happy but sad,
want to love but so mad,
will listen but can't hear,
smile with a tear.

The noise is loud,
the voices are quiet.
Don't want to be in the crowd
but can't stand being uninvited.

What do you want
from the world?
What can it offer?
Close your eyes

and decide
your fate.
Set the time,
it can't wait.

Alone on a bench
staring at her full image,
a recurring reminder
that her glow
once existed only for you.

Despite the craters
you left scarred
on her surface,
the light in her
will never dim.

Stars you chase
throughout your nights
are mere accessories
to the beauty
the moon can possess.

Just because she casts your shadow,
doesn't mean you should forget,
she, who exhales life into the moon,
cannot lose what she has never inhaled.
You.

He, who lies
about being a liar,
knows no truth.

He, who knows only fear,
grips tightly to his insecurities,
never filling the void.

He, who is lost,
is not placed in a lost and found,
he is, who is missing.

He, who is deceitful,
is a resident of a black hole,
tell me where he once resided.

He, he, he,
who is laughing,
is laughed at.

He, who is surrounded,
is lonely and searching,
for the path of the moon.

He sat in my living room teasing that he was going to head home, kissed my cheek, then kissed closer to the corner of my lips several times. He said it was an excuse to kiss my cheek. He subtly had me sit closer to him and gently kissed my cheek and corner of my lips again.

He went to the kitchen to get lemonade, walked back, telling me to stand up, saying "I love examining your body" and gently glided his hands on my collar bone, shoulders and arms. He started to kiss me so sweetly and then more passionately. He took my shirt off and slowly, very slowly unsnapped my bra, letting it fall down each arm. Kissing me intensely and biting my lips, he lifted me up and carried me to the bedroom, instructing me to undress him as he finished undressing me. Then telling me to get on the bed.

We had sex three times, each time he told me to kiss him, he was so good to my body. After the first time, he wanted to take a shower together. He grabbed my hand and kissed me all the way to the shower. He washed my back and conditioned my hair so gently. Touching my face and looking into my eyes as if time had stopped. Covering me with the towel once we had finished.

We sat in towels on the couch for a little while, he just held me so tight. Before eventually sleeping together a second and third time, we found ourselves lying in each other's arms and he was beginning to doze off. I wasn't sure if he planned on going home or would pass out here for the night.

He woke himself up, we began to talk and the mood changed. After some confusion, whether he was leaving or staying, he spent the night at my place. I didn't sleep the whole night.

Today, I want to end my life.

The distance of the sun
changes your perception
of its depth.

From here, he is a force,
a ball of ever-surviving light.
He is deceiving.

As you look in his direction,
blinds you with his energy,
warms you from afar.

Dare to make your way
in the vicinity of his aura
and he will set you to flames.

Tug of war,
competing
for the strength
possessed
by pride.

What are we
fighting for?
No substance
for the battles
we inflict
on ourselves.

Empty
is the path
on a blank map;
why do we
travel on separate roads?

Stay, just stay.
Your journey
should have ended
when you landed
on me.

You changed
my mind.
Awoke as you,
bled me out.

Open wounds
where I used to be,
scars displayed
for all to see.

You pour toxins,
further inflicting me
with your pain.
Transferring your weight.

All this time,
my fear slept
tucked in
by shadows
of the moon.

Left my guard
unattended,
basting in the sun.
Blindly burned,
scorned and scarred
by your rays.

Body cooked
from the inside
out.
"Stand in the shade,"
they said.

I laid out,
I baked,
dashed to shelter
when the sun fell,
lost in your light.

I lived hidden
from the night,
only to realize
it was the day
that was unjust;
cremation.

Emerged from the body
of deep blue sea,
finally escaping
intense pressure;
suffocation.

Suspended physically,
drowning emotionally,
draining realities
mentally.

Unstable,
submerged in
a gulf of your
wavering promises.

I came up for air,
in time to save
what was salvageable;
changing the tides
by lunar light.

Here is a story
for the old
and the young,
it's not about rainbows,
puppies or fun.

There once was a girl
who walked too close
to the sun.
She opened her eyes
and looked into the light,

Lost sight of her journey
and decided to run.
One would never believe
that this star gave such a chill;
dead in her tracks,
she stood very still.

For the sun could not warm her
and his image did not warn her;
it lured her into the cold
where he thought he could keep her;
to have and to hold her.

Unfortunately for him
he was not aware
of the fire in her heart
that his soul could not bear.
She was free in the dark.

"I don't want this nightmare to end,"
you told me as I attempted to loosen your grip.
I couldn't escape your hold on me.

They say it was abusive,
I say it was so attractive.
I was your possession.

Selfishly, I wanted to be
your only object of obsession.
Giving up my soul so selflessly,
selling myself to a demon.

If only your hard-on for control
had been just for me.
I would have given up so easily.

Bruised and broken,
I lie there, barely breathing.
You are gone.

Your weight lifted
from my chest;
still, I am gasping for air.

Dependent on your sharp tongue,
swift touch and endearing eyes,
I was lost with the stroke of your abuse.

I close my eyes
and I can see;
obliteration.

Destruction caused by crashing,
two powerful forces,
never meant to meet.

You loved my hatred for you.
I hated the way you loved.
Together, bound by the torment.

I sit in silence
refusing to admit
that my love
still exists.

Teardrops travel
through the paths
of my identity.
Is this Love?

I push emotions
way down to my toes,
where they tingle
far from my heart to feel.

My soul dismembered
from the wrath of Brinx.
The tornado that you are,
uplifted all that I am.

Forever changing
the who that I was.
You live inside me,
even though I have moved on.

Stitched wounds on this cardiac,
an endless reminder of what could have been.
How could I ever forget
the wrath that is Brinx?

His thirst for this venomous idolatry
seeps through the howls
called out to the night's full moon.

Time stands still for a man
who longs for lust
with the absence of affection.

Stillness, not a single beat from his heart,
the blood only journeys to his manhood.
Patience lives only in a man who loves.

A conflicting feeling,
sits in the pit of my stomach.
Reminiscing the way your arms
wrapped around me as if you believed
that you could never ever let me go.

Now I hate the hold hovering my waist,
the pain from that memory
has peeled several layers
from my now-dormant heart.
Why even keep me in your clutch?

The release of your pleasure
created an unescapable pressure.
I play that memory on loop,
over and over and over again,
viciously ripping my chest open.

I patch up my wounds each morning
only to bleed out every night.
Replaying and pinpointing the few,
and frankly, the only lasting impressions.
And even in rage, I still want you.

Even in such poor quality,
I keep searching for you
in my new encounters.
So uniquely unstable
with a beautiful facade.

You're 480p
in a 4K obsession,
yet my prized possession.
So unclear and misleading,
unpredictable but intriguing.

Leaving me curious,
licking my fingertips
to hold on to the taste.
I didn't see
the downgrade.

I've always been a hoarder,
never seeing the true value
or knowing when to take out the trash.

Remember when you said
sending nude photos
was like sending flowers?

We lived many months
in a floral shop.
I bared my body;

gave you my nudity,
stripping myself of all
that I kept from blooming.

I gave you flowers
every day that year
and you let them die.

The only time you loved me
was when I was leaving,
so I kept running away,
just to feel any reaction from you.

How many times
did I need to escape
for you to realize
you wanted me to stay?

Now I am running
but it is not from you;
it is from me,
to finally learn to love myself.

You taught me
to bury the pain
beneath the trees
beyond the core.

My biceps intercept
the soreness of my heart,
as I dig deeper
to hide my craving.

Let it slip through
these fingers
into the dirt.
Lay it to rest.

Body springs up
in the middle
of this king size
and you're gone.

Awoken by the reality
that I was the only one
who slept in this bed.
You were never here.

I dreamt of my love,
felt the warmth
of his body
in depths of my mind.

A figment
of my imagination,
I created you
from dust.

Never had the company
I thought I had kept.
Still awaking silent nights
with my loneliness.

When I start to feel,
I press the pen to paper,
disguise my whys
and mask the grief.

Alone with my despondency,
all I can do is shelter myself
by composing the words of my sorrow
rather than projecting my woes onto you.

The pages give back life
to the desolation of my soul.
And even so, I need you
as a muse to continue this transcript.

I hide between the space
of the light.
Coincidentally, it was
where I found you.

Searching for accessories,
not realizing
I was the main attraction.
You were smitten.

So I thought.

Every time our lips met,
I inhaled deeply,
every ounce of your soul.

My lungs filled to capacity;
holding you in,
leaving me breathless.

I died each time
yours pressed up
against mine.

Allowing you to enter
in all the ways
our bodies would consent.

To stop cherishing what you possess
will be my most difficult task.
It is death with or without you.

It wasn't the fact
that we didn't work
for each other;

It was YOU
who didn't put in work
for me.

Lungs completely deflated,
each day I gasp for your breath.

Missing your warm body
engulfing every inch of mine.

Pain seeps through my eyes;
tears run with blood.

Collapsing chest imploding
into a black hole sun.

Without the sun,
the moon takes on the darkness.

Hidden in the night
unseen, unknown and unloved.

Lack of love.
Lack of light.

Death to stars.
Death to night.

A new moon phase.
Your shaft of sunlight
buries behind my thighs;
"Don't open your eyes;"
enter the dark side.

You whisper
heat of passions
encasing my neck
as you focus that beam
in from behind me.

Eyes instructed shut,
awaiting your surprise.
Standing in the darkness,
feeling the warmth
of your fingertips;

digging into my back,
following the intensity
of your breath against my
shivering surface.
Take me.

Unable to escape
as your rays seep in,
deep down through
my cavernous crater.
Owned.

Is it really
selling your soul
if the exchange
is with your soulmate?

Am I giving up
on myself
by giving in
to you?

Indescribable,
yet unmistakable,
forces pull us together;
only to tear us apart.

Edible destruction,
feast your eyes
on me.
Dig in, you beast.

Love
or a cataclysmic
defeat?
Who decides?

I couldn't find peace
in my silence.
The sun doesn't shine
on a cloudy day.

Unsettled in this gloom,
anxiety bred a day too long.
I called out to light;
it excecated my mind.

Uncertain sentiments,
clear black and white
images of failure.
Undeniable denial.

Forecast forever
changes within
each space between time.
The sun dictates our lives.

The flame burning
under my vessel's layer
slowly losing its fire.

Heat that had once
resonated through depths
of my transparent ghost

has begun to cool down.
Brisk air progressively
solidifies the flow

that once ran free
through the plumbing
of this empty shell.

A beautiful death
of that dying breed.
Bitter silence.

Rest is for the weary,
requesting peace
is for the weak.

Scratching,
digging,
ripping,
skin.

Searching,
frantically,
vigorously
within.

Wanting,
needing,
craving
sin.

Can't
let
you
win.

Dancing flames
reflect on the iris
of my eyes.

What once was
wet with tears,
dried into fire.

These eyes
no longer sweat
for you.

She hates him.
Every word
escaping the hole
in his face
is hollow.

Empty pleas,
promises and proposals
dance in the smoke
he exhales.
He doesn't love her.

She inhales his tales,
vomiting his lies,
they are rejected
by her body.
She refuses to succumb.

His relentless attempts
are only echoes
of his vacant heart's
shell.

He knows no humanity.

How does he get
away
with this
attempted murder?

He is able to persuade
his way into innocence.
Killing the focus
and quality of her life.

Innocent until proven,
though, she is the only one
who can condemn him.
He has taken her will.

"Open your fucking legs"
as he restrained me in a chokehold.
"I'll make you feel better"
as he led me to my bedroom.

My temperature rose to 100.4,
with no regard to my health,
mentally or physically,
he took it from me.

Whispering, "It's too easy
to punish you, you're too weak
to fight back, it wouldn't be much fun."
Spread me wide open so he could just cum.

I said nothing, dazed and sedated,
from the meds I ingested,
without putting up a fight,
giving up and giving in.

He did not only take my body
that night, he stripped me of my dignity.
I allowed him to take his advantage,
he took the little I had left inside.

Leaving himself inside,
to swim between the tunnels
of my femininity.
He raped my soul without a thought.

Finally, I felt like an object,
no longer of his affection,
just a puppet in his show.
He pulled my strings for the last time.

I died on a frigid Wednesday evening,
body and mind had finally been broken,
just as he proposed many months before.
The one and only time he ever uttered truth.

Closing the door
on your uncertain face
was my greatest victory.

I had survived
the whirling tornado
of your destruction.

Your storm
would no longer destroy
my world.

You were no longer
a world I would desire
to possess.

Sigh, my love, my love,
my love was my own
and I will cherish myself.

Fore, I had projected
my passions onto thee,
only to have been in love

with me.

Worth of a warrior
can only be known
to the warrior at war.

Running through trenches,
in combat with darkness,
fighting for life.

Realizing this life
had a price
she was willing to pay.

The value of her soul
came with the cost
of selling his to her opponent.

Raising her hand
for the highest bid
to save herself from defeat.

Never born a princess
settling for less.
She was a soldier.

Day one was bliss.
No regard,
no responsibility.

Surpassing the first year,
the beginning
of the disguise.

Finishing up to year two,
no regard, no responsibility,
just regret.

Knock, knock, knock,
sounds echo from the door
alarming my solitude.

A cycle of your return,
running on a wheel
chasing destructive emotions.

We cannot be cured,
we don't want to commit,
yet, it's impossible to be apart.

You weigh comfort versus love.
I weigh freedom versus narcissism.
How could this not end in war?

You love on conditions,
terms and fiction.
Convincing yourself I'm not the one.

I am the one.
You know it.
I know it.

Words of "I hate you"
mean nothing to you,
once you look into my eyes.

We are both such good liars.
You lie to keep me.
I lie to push you away.

She doesn't know me,
how can I expect her to?
I think about her
as much as I think of him.

Trying from three angles
to shape up this love
but facing opposite directions.

He hides me from her,
she turns a blind eye
of his addiction to us.
He no longer hides her.

I don't know her
even though loving him
shows me who she might be.
What is the difference between

her,
him
and
me?

We are enemies
on the same team
loving, holding, caring
for the same man.

Instead of helping
each other seek truth,
we hide behind the lies,
nesting in our own denial.

He's been inside me,
inside her,
leaving his genes
in our pools.

Yet we still choose
to fight for his affection.
He loves it.
Feeding his ego.

Bird seed to the man
who waits for his next meal;
day in and day out.
We always fill his appetite.

Tumult of emotions,
we are violent agitations
of passion.

Our forces collide
rapidly, as if we were to die
in this instant.

Rushing into each other,
our bodies cry out,
in agony and in pleasure.

You bite into my lips,
my hips, my ribs, my thighs;
ripping into my mind, my body.

Distinctively staring through you,
uncovering, exposing and stripping
your every layer, hoarding all of you.

We will devour each other,
feeding off our chemistry,
oozing from voids of our beings.

Administering your body,
as you dominate every inch of mine.
Who is really governing who?

On this very day,
you emerged into life.

On this very day,
you endured pain, power and strife.

On this very day,
you realized you were alive.

On this very day,
a path was made for you to drive.

On this very day,
thirty years from then,

you have grown up to be
one of many men;

to see the light from glowing eyes,
to take the risk; to finally fly.

On this very day,
the journey of a man was born.

When a relationship ends,
memories flash before your eyes,
like you are on your deathbed.

For some, pleasant clips
play as you mourn the loss
of all the smiles and laughter.

For others, suspenseful, horrific
flashbacks give you chills,
making you wonder how it ever was.

Nonetheless, you experience deprivation
of a counterpart who once held you
and a love's potential.

I've become so accustomed
to the pain you disguise
as love, I am too exhausted
to decipher between the two.

I wrestled the thoughts
that combat in my mind.

Have you ever cried without the tears?
You feel your body buried in heartache
but your eyes run dry. Why?

Is this what it is to feel numb?
Or my excuse for hugging the denial
just so I can hold onto some crumbs.

Do you know what it feels like to starve?
You are mentally and physically deprived
of all the fuel you owe to yourself.

Can you feel my heart beating?
I haven't felt a thump in my chest
since my love fell on deaf ears and blind eyes.

She is the only image
of love that truly
serves him.

She is lost in him,
without reason;
neglects herself.

She needs,
no, she wants, no,
needs him, no, help.

She is tangled
in his web of lies;
waits for partial truths.

She hangs herself
from a noose; no,
dangles from puppet strings.

She serves him.
She neglects herself.
She needs him, no, help.
She waits for partial truths.
She dangles from puppet strings.

Your subtle attempts
to control my behavior
have worn me thin.

Threats of building a wall
to shut out the noise
that prohibits your comfortability

to destroy me.
I dare you to build a wall
so high that you cannot climb over.

When you feel like you have lost
power and the means to dominate,
I beg you to stay behind that wall.

Do not threaten me with your emptiness,
your lack of conviction
used to keep your flock following you.

You are not a shepherd,
nor a leader.
Your walls are weak.

Shut down,
I beg of you.
Build that wall.

Standing here,
second in line,
I don't want
to be number two.

I am not a bowel movement
taken when necessary
to release and unleash
the toxins of your being.

My acceptance
to being second
has led me to
place myself third.

To you,
then to her.
You continuously
shit all over me.

Resigning to your toxicity
has only strengthened
who I am meant to be.

You are a wrecking ball,
compiled of roots
that fuel your demolition.

I feed off your ruination,
powering me to become
a wolf in the night.

Howling as the moon
shines full of my own
control.

You
will
not
win.

There's this overwhelming weight
that sits on my chest
when I loved someone
who would not love me back.

The heaviness in my heart,
feels like it's been submerged in water
being a victim of his lovebombing.
I was drowning in his false affections.

"He doesn't love you!" They said,
over and over.
"But I know that he does!" I said,
over and over.

And he didn't. I found out
after I gave him all the hope
I ever had in me to possess.
It's too late.

"I don't love him!" I cry out.
No one believes me.
"But I really do love her!" He persists.
No one believes him.

The lines are smeared
under all the lies,
we flooded every boundary,
inundated within depths of my tears.

What a shame,
a disservice,
to yourself,
pushing me away.

It was more of risk
to lose me than it was
to keep me
but your hunger for attention

and insecurities bowing down
to the fixation of reassurance
from nameless faces
weighed heavy on your scale.

You are the ruination
of yourself.
Self-condemning
with unnecessary deprivations.

Using your weapon
as an excuse,
playing the poor victim
to assault minds of the innocent.

Guiltless actions,
day in and day out,
not worth correcting
your selfish tunnel vision.

I drowned in an ocean
of my own tears.

I was so in love
with your mythology.

A Hera to my Zeus.
It was Greek to me.

Blinded by your stories,
I closed my eyes as I read.

You were unbelievable
and I still believed you.

What a tale,
I will tell.

To be in love with the devil,
I never thought I'd fall for sin.

Disguised his eyes
with a cloak of purity.

I dove headfirst
into the gates of hell.

Mesmerized by the heat,
I didn't want to cool down.

Covering my body
with a blanket of evil.

Still believing
he was my savior.

This pulsating lump
thumping in my chest
needs you.

Beat me, bruise me,
hurt me, pull me,
squeeze me, bite me.

Let your teeth sink
deep into my soul.
Eat me inside out.

Indulge in the disaster.
Hold on tight.
We keep moving.

There is no stopping this fire.
I am burning myself alive
to keep you warm.

Craving
interferes
with sanity.

Crazy for your
love?
Lust?

Supply me,
fuel me,
destroy me.

I can take it.
You do take it.
It is yours.

Sold my soul,
surrendered myself
to you.

I'm stuck in a forever
of misleading expectations.
Chasing my tail,
expecting another body
connected to it.

Still me,
try again.
Wait, no,
still me.
Again.

Raised in a world
of guidelines to follow.
Step by step,
just follow this path
of unrealistic outcomes.

I thought life
was an equation,
you add, you subtract,
sure to achieve the equal.
I am terrible at math.

Wasn't there supposed to be
a formula to my achievements?
"Supposed to be"
equals
entitlement.

Mathematical error
number one.
Solve the equation:
if you are not entitled,
what are you?

I never found that answer,
added too much,
subtracted too little.
Ended up with more problems
and a zero.

Like Snow White
running from the huntsman,
I am swatting away the creatures
of the night.

Lost in the darkness,
I can't seem to find the light.
Always feel like I am escaping
evil,

only to find out
that I am avoiding
contact with myself.
Denial.

Palm to my face
alerting the tears
to shoot from my eyes.
It's okay during sex, right?

A craving for painful pleasure
was always my thing
until it became just painful.
How can I go back now?

Go slow, please ease into it.
Ramming yourself into me anyway.
"This leg is pissing me off,
keep it there or I'll break it."

He can hear me whimper, fearfully
for the sake of my body,
"Wait, no, no, no, slow, slow, slow."
Deeper and deeper, down into darkness.

When it was over, I had to pretend
that I liked it, that I liked you.
Holding back the tears when you asked,
"Hey, you okay? Let me see your face."

I can't put my finger
on the feelings I don't have
anymore.

The concrete hugs my ankles
in this puddle of mud.
Stuck.

Not trying hard enough
to break away from the mold.
Complacent.

I can't sit.
I can't lay.
Standstill.

Light peeks in through the window
from other homes full of life.
It shines upon the darkness
that blankets us both in this bed.

The moon doesn't look the same
to me anymore. Just a cold glowing rock.
I can't even lie there peacefully in love,
there is much work to do, putting you to sleep.

Unable to rest until you are dreaming
because you whisper, "Show your daddy love
and pick my back, put daddy to bed."
I force myself awake until you breathe heavily.

Some nights, I can't make it for too long,
I disappoint you, you can't sleep,
especially if I am sleeping.
So you wake me up any way that you can.

It's been a year since I've had a good night's rest.
Tucking you in or weathering long hours with you
and your restless mind.
We work really hard for your nightly rejuvenation.

I am exhausted as you softly call to me,
"My love, put those hands on me, I really need
to sleep tonight." I silently take a deep breath
as I feel my soul begin to weep.

Not once in the last year that we have shared a bed
did he tuck me in and lay me to rest.
When he whispers, "My love," I cringe
knowing the truth is, he is My Love, I, his servant.

Every single day,
it's the same story.
You dictate,
I record.

I hang on every word,
waiting for you to write
me a love sonnet
or just a happy ending.

Your ink stains
every layer of my skin.
Branded by your abuse,
tattooed on my soul.

I need this tale
you tell
to end,
before I do.

Nestled in your embrace was powerful,
never knowing I had always been a source of your control.
It all began with the induction of lust,
masked so gracefully as intensified love.
An addiction delivered by your demon,
only appearing under the light of the moon.

One clear night, our eyes shared a glimpse of the moon.
That moment was ever so notable and powerful.
I slept countless nights with the son of a demon.
This distinct aura seeped from your pores, taking my control,
disguised as the brilliant and convincing façade of love.
Tightly latching onto my soul with this lust.

Our energies were bonded, giving immediate permissions to lust,
desperate souls bound together, inhaled by the breath of the moon,
mistaken for all the innocence and purities of this imitation of love.
The link joining us strengthened you to become more powerful.
Yearning and craving the sensual satisfaction of this control;
to feed all you thought needed to be fed to your demon.

There, lives in you, the vital force of a demon;
driven by addictions of intense and destructive lust.
Authorizing you a false sense of control
while hiding on the dark side of the moon.
Raising a monster to hunger to be more powerful,
unaware of the undeniable distraction called love.

You question my ability to love
for the lust had lost its shine to this demon.
It deemed itself the need to be more powerful
starving for something deeper than lust;
searching in the night while wolves howl at the moon.
You began to feel the slip of your control,

Dismembering all aspects of what you thought was in your control;
being served all the pains and consequences of disparaging love.
An unforgiving light cast upon your darkness beneath the moon.
Dear boy, you are no longer a separate entity from your demon.
You continuously long for an unattainable lust,
and you will never achieve a life that is powerful.

www.ingramcontent.com/pod-product-compliance
Lightning Source LLC
LaVergne TN
LVHW051426080426
835508LV00022B/3255